The Few

but

The Heavy

Book II

JETHRO SHEIKH SPEAR

The Few
but
The Heavy
Book II

© Jethro Sheikh Spear

First published: March 2016

ISBN 978-9976-89-595-7

Published by;

J. S. SpeaR

CONTENTS

THIS PAGE WAS LEFT OUT INTENTIONALLY

CHAPTER ONE: THOUGHTFUL OR INSPIRATIONAL

THE SPIRIT

The literal meaning of a Spartan is a citizen of Sparta, a Greece but the implementation is any person with a firm heart, who has no softness and doesn't tolerate weaknesses,

A warrior in within has courage bigger than the muscles

Every significant, positive change was made from the choice done by a courageous heart which later spread to many to achieve a large scale change

An important notice is that, each big thing started from a small one

And this particular small thing comes from smaller number or even a single person who must always be the warrior in within

But one must wonder what does it take to build a warrior in oneself?

Begin by embracing your strong side; practicing firmness to what you know is true opens doors to great accomplishments ahead of you

But live in no lie, the truth is, the greater the accomplishments the harder the tasks and not the other way around

The beginning of almost any great future is a difficult past

The road to heaven is rougher than the road to hell

As it is said, when things get tough, only the tough gets going

Life challenges behave like test, you are the tested but the funny thing is the judge is life itself

But to pass the test, as much as knowledge is required it is the same way guts are required, the guts that we shall always remember is what makes a warrior true

Some multimillion companies began with a capital of about 1000 USD; to reach that goal it takes years, falls, regrets but most importantly patience

It takes few to reach there because few actually believe in reaching there

That is why it is wisely said; only those risking going far can know how far they can go

It is a simple fact on its own
elegance, how can you really ever find
out if you don't find out?

But no matter how much I tell you that
you can do it, I must be honest that
only you can let yourself do it

Today is today, tomorrow is indeed
another day.

There no better opportunity than now
but bear it in mind tomorrow is a today
just not yet

Patience builds tolerance, tolerance
advances patience but to achieve that
your heart needs to be pure as your
minds is determined

When the fear grows in your heart
making it race like a panting dog,
trembling as your adrenaline cannot
decide whether you should fright or you
should fly

Take a deep breath, remember your lord,
remind yourself of what you are, what
you are doing and what it will get you
and bravely keep moving forward because
fear can only be solved by facing it
and inspiration merely seduce it

You are what you are and yet you aren't
what you are

You are weak right now and that is what
you let yourself be and that becomes of
you

You aren't truly weak but strong and
since you are still struggling to do it
be it in your heart that proves it you
are

Gloriously attempts to greatness shows
no mercy to what weakens you

Your weakness is your enemy

And a weakness is no longer a weakness
when you know it, it becomes laziness

If laziness is your weakness, you are
your own weakness

Work hard, stay focused, think straight
and stay firm to the truth

To be brave doesn't mean to be inhuman
or mean rather it means to keep moving
forward no matter how scared you are

Be a Spartan

LITTLE LIGHT ON LIFE

Marriage is boring because spouses are boring

Marriage and love has the same goal of peace, it is us that abuse them by choosing to believe the adventure in them is over just because those that we wanted we have them

How can life be not important not to talk about? It is the most important discussion even if you were living on the moon

And due to such life is the most common experience of all to all of us still very few are experts of living

Because surviving is just to ensure you don't die and get the things you want in time, living is finding purpose in the good you do

To have good life isn't about having fortune but it is about having things of satisfaction

And satisfaction isn't a material, it is something earned by heart due to excellence in morality

Let our minds invent the cars but it
will be our hearts that tell us where
to drive them to

Love isn't a bad thing no matter how
bad is everyone

Because without it, how would people
have mercy over other people whom they
aren't related to?

And it shall always be true that love
is bigger than logic

Trust builds love and friendship is all
about trust

If you don't trust your friend, think
of another name for him or her

Those who keep waiting for tomorrow
they never live their today

Time isn't your slave, you cannot order
him the way you want

For a fact being good to yourself alone
makes you bad to people

If you are good to people it makes you
good to yourself

I tell you my dear friend fear God and
love him

Because only the fearing of God and
loving him could mean the same thing
but the rest shall never be so

POETIC CLARITY

The master creation of God is as
beautiful as it is sufficient

As for our beautiful home, he designed
it just for us to dwell in it

And the cleverness of some men have
made that beauty prosper

Such gift of human thinking has made
our living easier

Not the thinking of evil that brings
another effect to our lives

Ideas that disobeys the laws of our
creator

The misuse of others brilliance reveals
the lies beneath our claims when we
create weapons to kill each other

And so it for a fact history is written
by the blood of common men

Death of men in the name of their
countries doesn't justify the sacrifice

And men who sent them to their deaths
are named patriots

While the enemy sees them as villains,
we shall decorate them as heroes, such
a mad world

In the very name some men don't get to
see their sons become men as well

It is the sad story only the low class
people can truly tell, the kind of pain
that is nearly impossible to endure

It is by the same deceit more money
will be spent for potential mass
destruction and yet sad children are
starving

While other children are left with no
choice than to be soldiers

It is a shame how human desire for fame
and luxury could prove purposeless in
life

Or in arrogance of personal looks while
another one struggles to enjoy their
incompleteness

They will spend their entire lives
having hard time believing they are
beautiful or at least they could be

The blind eye men can play on others
suffering shows how mischievous men can
be

We inflict pain over one another or
never try to stop others' pain and
later in round tables discussing if it
is God's fault

If you want peace on earth, be the
peace you wish to see in the world

***Inspired by Gandhi's famous quote be
the changes that you want to see in the
world***

FRIENDS Vs LOVERS

It is common for lovers to firstly be friends but what is exceptional is for them to stay as friends while they are lovers

Such is a task only by excellent morals, adjustment, a non-egoistic nature and patience can make it happen

Love that is birthed after marriage is only of condition to be conceived before it

To be pleased to live with someone else is the conceived love, only till then it becomes the birthed one

And for the love before marriage is real but not to be relied upon because character is a necessary credit for it

If you were lovers and ended your relationship by deciding to be friends, unless there was no love it can stay that way unaffected but otherwise the topic of love always come in

Because for such situation, the basic problem is either the fear for the future or the need for no commitment

For those people who become lovers
again that is because they simply
wanted to take a break

The most adventurous relationship is
the relationship that lies between
lovers and friends

It is always with flattering, caring
and consuming into obsession if not
switched to love any soon

And by relationship between lovers and
friends it doesn't mean your boyfriend
or girlfriend

It means that person you call your
friend and you love to flirt with, be
with and sometimes you call him or her
your best friend only to cover the
truth in your heart

You enjoy her or his company far more
than your same sex friends and you can
make each other smile in a way nobody
does

These kinds of people they may not be
our first priority but they have the
priority much enough to shake the first
priority

This relationship is most favorable to
players because they can get what they
want unquestioned

When you go through this relationship
and you are of somebody else, you will
not easily introduce that person to
your actual partner

Though they aren't rivals officially,
you know in your heart that they are

Don't be surprised if they have the
exactly thing missing in your partner
be it the looks or the charms but not
money because that doesn't count

You shall know it well if you were
alone, somewhere just the two of you

You know that anything can happen and
still you didn't take any precautions

And suppose it happens, guilt and
happiness will mix up to form a complex
feeling that you fail to give it a name
for some time

The harder you try to find the answer,
the more it consumes you

It might have been a crush last week,
obsession next week but today it is
love or just a disease if not taken
care of.

*inspired by the book; THE THREES OF
RELATIONSHIPS by Jethro Sheikh Spear*

TIME TO ACT

You have inspired yourself countless despite the fact that you were heart moving, you have countless broken your heart as well

A person who has all that is required to achieve a goal even with lesser components yet does nothing is the greatest disappointment he or she will ever face

It isn't always about money or chance to achieve your dreams but sometimes it simply about the will power

But if it is about chance then create it, if it is about money seek it, if it is about time wait for it

But in either way of whatever way, your excuses are blunt

Having fear or procrastinate to what you rightfully have to do simply because you are scared or you think there is tomorrow at each step of your life you will make no difference with a person who isn't even visionary as you are

The moment you thought of it, schemed
it that is moment you were ready

Sometimes waiting for a more right
moment is the wisest decision while
waiting you are ready but you are just
buying some time so it may be most fit
to do it

It is time to stop saying you can and
get it done

It is time to stop saying you are
clever or talented and get it proved

A moment in a man's life can leave an
impact in history

Don't underestimate a minute; an hour
or a day for an Olympic record is made
within counts of few seconds

Believing in what you can do isn't what
you can do

The thought is in the head, until you
let it out you too don't know what you
can do

Stand up and stay up

Legend is ready to be written and your
next action determines the next words

Speak to your soul about your dreams

It was once said; don't dream of small
dreams for they have no power to move
the hearts of men

And you are not a small dreamer

ALL WE HAVE IS A CHOICE

There are two things that happen for certain in life, the fact it is life and the fact it will one day not be life anymore.

The details between life and death shall fill memories only by the virtue of what we chose, destiny or not, it is what we choose.

No one breaks your heart except the one you love but no one breaks your spirit except you have left them to do so.

The brave heart shall try not to drop a tear but the strong soul shall move on even if it were to cry a river.

A man's story is only important by what he succeeds and let's be honest, when has great story filled with easy choices?

In the street we shall feel the bitter weather; in the home we shall feel the unwelcome solitude of loneliness, we can say the governments don't care or we shall govern ourselves like we don't care

Before you make it the closest people will attempt to break you first, they will be the ones to tell you that you can't do it, be it in the whispers behind your back or in front of your face but it is a choice to listen to the one person who will have even a little faith in you or the ones who don't

But how can you stop to do what you must, it is like to make a child not cry while is in pain only the adults can choose not to cry

Here is the fact, as far as it isn't wrong you have the right to want but choose carefully what you choose to want because it is what you want that will make you right or wrong

Before we are blessed to do what we want, we got to do what we must. There is no choice to that than the choice to choose if you really want it or not

Pull a trigger that is an action but to what the bullet will do isn't in your hands

The point we have no choice is when we chose to believe we have no other choice but that's the choice we made

But where is the choice in seeing a
great opportunity or blessed with great
capacity to deliver a specific enquiry?
Possibly the kind only you can, where
is the choice?

Oh yah, there is a choice, do it or
stay there for someone else to do it

There is fire and water, east and west
and by fact good and bad, that is the
number one right

When you stop for a while and look
back, life is amazing or just terrible

One thinks of it as a lesson and
another hates God for it

When one sees the moon hanging says it
is gravity another one says it is God's
doing, one appoints the mechanism as
the answer another one points the
mechanic who made the mechanism

Choose fanatically, dwell on yesterday
or tomorrow either way you do that
today

It is your destiny I know but careful
there, until every turn has lead you to
that turn, don't call it anything but a
choice

And when the choice makes sense yes
call it destiny because the story makes
sense at the last chapter

OUR HOMES

If there is amount of truth about life
then it is mysterious but of all the
mysteries in life the most strange of
all is love

In life you jump from careers to
careers, from jobs to jobs to find that
one thing that suits you and is worth
doing forever.

Whereas in life doing so makes you
stronger and experienced, in love it is
seriously the opposite. Jumping from
one relationship to the other makes our
ability to love weaker and the so
called experience means nothing when
you fall in love again.

The best way is to avoid being in a
relationship if you are afraid he or
she isn't the one.

But you haven't been in love if you can
do that because when you meet someone
it always feels is the one no matter
how much life turns to prove otherwise

If you are in love and can stand to
resist it by some caution, two things
could happen, you are going to go
through pain before you have her or him

or you going to lose him or her because they cannot wait forever.

Either you keep engaging with wrong people or resist the right one over the years you lose faith in love but yet you love again, you do that often until you begin to think it has no meaning at all, and when you let yourself believe that, then you have failed the test of true love.

How do we know when it is right? Will the sun stand still for days? Will our hearts go silently in love finding ourselves in their arms already or we shall notice all by the tense heart beats due to the adrenaline?

How can we ever know when we find the ones?

Some tells us of stories of people they have been with, bearing their faults believing no one is perfect and so we should learn to find the compatibility

Some tell us of stories of wild friends who are so alike and that their alikeness is love

Whereas some tell us of the principle opposite charges attract to mean the one for you isn't like you but the opposite

This puzzle requires you to be careful enough to decide someone to go through with the toughest experiences in life such like wondering why him or her of all people in the world or the most wonderful experiences like bringing a human being to life and raise it.

Just like business, when we have loss today and challenges yesterday it doesn't make us quit, why do we do so with love?

The idea of happiness is somewhere is from the human passion for adventure; we most often place it in the wrong place.

Unlike our homes we grew up with our families it is easy to go back, unlike finding a suitable career give it time you will find it but our homes for our hearts aren't places we grew up or places we can find because we persist.

Some people are lucky to find happiness with their first ones, some strangers they never even imagined but despite we can decide who to be with, we don't decide knowing them, meeting them or falling for them however we can decide

to deny the feelings or denying being
with them.

And when you decide to be with someone
no way is better to commit than
matrimony where there love is tested,
patience is proved and home is found,
the home for a heart.

***inspired by the book; THE THREES OF
RELATIONSHIPS by Jethro Sheikh Spear***

LET'S FIND THE EDGE

We shall say no further on the
predicament of our beginnings

We shall reside deeper in the promises
of the coming

Soon or later, we shall be content

A ruthless mind to its soul and body

We shall laugh not to our misbehaving
bodies

We shall not entertain the seduction of
our souls

But there the heart will lead, the mind
will command and the journey will
proceed

Till it reaches a point we have lost
unnecessary cautions called fear

Till we have lost unnecessary attention
that brings doubt

We shall reside in that and find homage

And before we know it

We shall have crossed the line of our
own expectations

INTERGRITY

I may not have done the impossible but
I can think of them

I may not have proved it but I do
believe in it

You may copy my ideas but you cannot
copy my mind

You may fail to master me while it is
me you don't understand

I am not an alien, I am merely a man

I am not a superstar; I am not at least
my own fan

What I do is the reciprocal of what I
believe I can do

What I believe I can do is the fraction
of what I can do

I know so little of what my lord has
blessed me with yet it amazes the minds
of men with wonder

I am ashamed to claim being
extraordinary to fell men, I am proud
of the ability to yield them
(extraordinary things)

It is not what I think that amazes me
but it is how

I though believe how is not essential
to men than what

I am just a son of man, how can I
pretend a shadow of God?

I do believe super heroes aren't by
their physical strength but the will
power

The strength of the mind and the beauty
of the heart

I have dreamt of being legend but
legend hasn't met me yet

It isn't about the fame; it is about
acknowledging the possibilities of the
coming

It is true, what will the world miss
with my absence but I intend to make it
false that nothing happened in my
presence

I have longed stopped worrying what
people presume of me

Men believe what they want to believe

Most humans hardly think I have
reserved myself from their comments

Unless it is from a pious or a wise
person, I surely open myself to be
judged

Today, today I have told myself it is
the last day to live the life of delay

I appreciate compliments but I fear to
believe them

What I think of my abilities could be
smaller than what people see

But I love my short sights on this
matter

Because I rather see myself big in my
world but small in others

I believe in being accountable to
people than people being accountable to
me

I rephrase the voice inside me since
when I knew me and that is as long as I
have been me

I was born a thinker but I didn't
become a thinker until a thinker was
born in me

And to the world I won't become a
thinker until a thinker is born out of
me

CHAPTER TWO:
LOVE/ROMANTIC

A DEDICATION

Everybody could mean it when they say
you are beautiful but none can mean it
like me when I say I love you

What they call your bodily imperfection
actually makes me crazy for you

The details over details about
everything about you is what makes my
thoughts over you blissful

I will be the first man in the world to
want what he already has because I just
cannot get enough of you

Did I tell you my heart races wherever
I meet with you? Did I tell you on our
first date I showed up with fever? Did
I tell you my heart calms wherever I
kiss you?

You are my superstar, my only celebrity

You give my life wonder, to impress you
it demands creativity

No matter how the world tries to take
me down, you are always my serenity

And I will always say your paint is
more worth than that of Monalisa and
that makes me a better Da vinci.

We are like portraits that represent
unsung history

A beautiful love story greater than the
myth of the old Greece

I will match you in the better lives
that we shall restfully share; being
with you is an incomparable opportunity

Our lives together is my world, the
good and the bad and all there is

Our world is vast than that of the
Roman Empire

And our love is immortal than any
vampire

You are the all beauties, be it snow
white or Cinderella

We may not be in books but our love is
worth a tale like that of Caesar and
Cleopatra

Let nobody tell you this isn't for
real, we just got started and there are
no sayonara

For our love I hope you fight like some
real freedom fighter

Don't worry; I intend to call you my
Sarafina

For the sun rays and rains, I am your
umbrella

You remind me how Darwin was wrong;
damn, could you have evolved from a
gorilla

You are so sweet, sweeter than coca
cola

You are so valuable, valuable than any
dollar

You are my energy source; God has made
you my solar

There might be few arguments, promise
me to be a sustainer

The last thing we need is a dilemma

Don't go away while I want you to stay,
it will cause heart fractures

While I still account you to make me
great as Alexander

Don't dare to replace me ever, let
forth to the last of time I be no to
you as a foreigner

And for the stunt you have cost my
heart, I dedicate this to you my dear

THEY ARE TRAPS

You are irresistibly beautiful that
their hearts quakes

So they wonder how you are my babe

And they would like to think you are a
piece of cake

Cheap enough that anyone can take

Please my love, show them how that is a
mistake

They play charming while they are
snakes

They play caring and cool while they
are fakes

They only want to spot your weaknesses
and have them naked

Before they have your heart at its
greatest break

They will play your body and say it is
love they make

That is why I am here to make sure you
don't shake

They are simply the rivers and I am the
lake

They are small minds still asleep while
I am long awake

Love is shown by actions not
advertisements

That is why I am showing you the right
way while they show you toys to
manipulate

They will suggest I am not worth of
you, please don't cooperate

Most don't know love, they only know to
fornicate

While I have given you what is beyond
sight, I have given you what could make
you easily sleep at night

You have seen already my girl; I am the
kind that can offer you an apology
before the fight

I am the kind that can make everything
around you colorful and not black and
white

So you may never have to decide if you
have to leave me for those jerks

So you may love me just a little bit
more and not as less as that

Because with that I am afraid one day
you may say me I love you and add the
word 'but'

At the moment you let yourself so weak
and just break my heart

Trust me I will be proud that I will
have not caused yours not even a
scratch

So listen to me once again baby, I am
good not because I cannot play dirt

I have chosen to love you truly without
an act
I love you regardless you are slim or
you will ever be fat

And not at all that your charms have
the best of art

You must understand what to do is must

Like how you got into my heart without
my mind to consult

I insist babes, if you won't let them
underestimate you I will show you how
much I have done is a mere start

FAVORITE DISEASE

I may be young to make many promises
but I am grown enough to fall in love

So give me a chance to explain I
promise not to waste your time

For all this time that I have been
waiting for you it has been feeling
like waiting for the only train

And you are so away, so unaware how
this washes my brain

Maybe you don't know me so well neither
do I know you that much, let's just say
love is as crazy as insane.

It defies all the good reasons but we
keep giving it a way

I have seen you in my head when upon
your lips I laid mine

I had in mind how beautiful it will be
when you rest on my chest, where I
could tell you that you are the finest

I have gone through some bearable pain,
believe me being in need of your love
isn't the sort I can sustain

Because it breaks my heart without a
touch, oh please untie me from this
chain

My will, my will is lighter and this
love is very dense, as how these
feelings are so intense for your love I
am determined

Determined to go far lengths

Just at least in a day let me see your
face

Just at least in a life time let me
have your kiss

If I won't, my death isn't worth 'rest
in peace'

Believe me, you are meant to make my
life complete

Because you are very nice, too much
sweet without you happiness is a deceit

If I could be able to see you, maybe I
would been on my knees

Though I don't expect to make you
believe so let me just tell you how
loving you is my favorite disease

I put a lot of time to think about you
during the day

I sometimes just want time alone so I
can think about you straighter

I make the same answers every day but
each time I do it feels like it is
reveled

When I am about to sleep at night, I
close my eyes though I don't see you
precise, you are as beautiful as I saw
you once in a time

I even wonder why people buy sleeping
pills while I simply imagine we are
dancing under the rain

And I relax and forget all the
misfortunes I had in my day as soon as
that I shall fall asleep

I am worried if you are aware but I
have been trying to be friends with
your friends

I put on my best; I suspect they will
tell you how impressive I am

You are my best talk to my friends;
they think I am paranoid

And that girl that likes me wishes I
were doing this to her

But I only see you, buffed with time,
careless of their opinions and you are
yet not mine and I still go on

That is how you are my favorite disease

41 | Page

GIVE ME TIME

I admit I feel drawn to you, I confess
I massively like you

Not even my most resisting state can
deny what I feel for you

I think about you, you are becoming a
behavior that is addictive

Every day that pass it cannot be well
if you don't even say Hi to me

Give me time to admit it is love
because I am not ready for any whiles
that may makes love painful

Don't mind me being defensive, you are
such handsome but I don't want you to
become irresistible because of your
face

But only because it is destined to be

I am glad you don't push me away; I am
assuming it is because you feel the
love truly

I love you maybe; I want you and that
is true

It is so easy for me to be completely
yours but all I need is the guarantee
you will fully be mine

I don't want to enlist you among my
exes

If you become mine, I would want you
for the rest of my life and for the
rest of yours

If it is love that is our fate, I want
us to be soul mates

Where you could still love me while you
know my worst, where you could treat me
as your best

I need truthfulness and to be honest
lies destroy a relationship as quick as
early

I may be in love with you but I need to
know you aren't here to make a fool out
of me

Let me be your solely partner, don't be
the kind that forsake me for the desire
to be free as if my company caves

I want to see you can switch yourself
for me

They say boys would want girls to do
crazy things for them and girls want
crazy boys to do decent things for them

If by crazy they mean love, sure I can
be crazy for you but I want you decent

enough that I know I chose the right
parent for my children

Part of me doesn't want to be with you
because you are too good to be true

In the way you love me, I have never
seen it before it is as if it is
impossible for you to give up

And your presentable personality would
make any girl beg you for your love and
just it; you are too good to be true

It isn't that I cannot learn to love
you but it is that what if I turn to be
a disappointment?

What if I am not good as you think of
me?

But no matter what I say, when you go
silent I miss you so much

When you come back I fear to welcome
you so close because I don't want to
give you false hope

But whatever the case I am in love,
hold a little longer and I shall fall
into your trap

Be my love I shall be your wife. Let me
be your only one and I will be the
rarest of the kind

I love you potentially; prove it and I
shall love realistically

THE LOVE OF MY LIFE

Your eyes, your eyes make me run out of
lies and yet they make me a giant of
lines

My heart goes bumpy, your lips goes
widely, I am happy when you are happy

My love, love is what I feel for you;
don't treat me as your option while I
treat you as my choice

You are the one I have opened my heart
to, hear my voice even if you as far as
across the ocean

Dress like a princess, life is short,
the future is unknown, let me fall deep
for you today, I don't want to hear any
doubts from you tomorrow

While I will be busy attending the
rehabs of this love addiction

I love your childish looks and your
sense of maturity

It is like I am drawn to a beautiful
book that I underestimated its power of
clarity

And I am aware there is no such thing
as a perfect woman but you have taught
me you are the right one

For the moon and the light, the sun and
the fire it burns

For the angels in the sky and the
beautiful birds in which they fly

You are a better ornament that which I
shall stand still forever surprised

When that day you cried before me just
by knowing I will be away for some
days, I have never felt so loved

And under the sun we rested whispering
words of love and promise to last
forever

My heart shall have to stop first
before you actually walk out of it

Never have I let my tears drop for a
woman but you made me cry like I lost
my mom

With no shame we did it together over
nothing but fearing that someday, we
may unfortunately have to take
different paths

It is true I am free of lies, your
presences raises my sense of
responsibility

The desire to have you a better future
has made me automatically a brighter
man

And nothing, nothing has made me work
than the desire to fulfill all your
wishes

Sometimes I don't just say it all not
for the sake of surprise but fearing I
may not be able to live up to it

So I spend more time working hard so
that later I may spend more time making
you the happiest woman on earth

Do you remember how anxious we were to
meet for the first time? Do you
remember how early we woke up for it
and yet all night we were awake
thinking of how it will be?

Mark my words, if this is not love I,
from this day name it so

And the best thing about all this is
that the past is a glorifying memory
but the future is more promising

It will be normal for me to be used to
you but I swear, I swear you have never
been normal to me not even for a single
minute

I would like to see you all the time
and in time when things are settled I
will be seeing you all I can

But I have a very strong feeling that I
shall yet not be satisfied

Not because you are an astonishing
beauty but because looking at you I
shall always keep in mind you must be
the love of my life

I am grateful I am under your care, I
am blessed to experience all this with
you

Your eyes, your eyes make me run out of
lies and yet they make me a giant of
lines

My heart goes bumpy, your lips goes
widely, I am happy when you are happy

HAVE ME A CHANCE

I don't mind if you think I am a silent
killer but if you choose to think so,
and then think of me as your only
musketeer

Welcome me in your heart I shall forth
cause you no tears, only those of joy
of course because your happiness is
what I shall procure

I am a doctor before I went to medical
school; I am destined to make you well
my love is such a blessed cure

I am such a fire that is cool; I will
warm you when you are cold, cool you
when you are hot and when you need the
moderate I will be there for sure

So don't mistake me for a fool, in
tasks of love I am both the thinker and
the doer

If you are snow white then I am the
prince charming, huntsman and even all
the seven dwarfs

If our lives are like twilight, I shall
be the hybrid of the both the vampire
and the werewolf

All that just to be the only one for
your affection with absolute no
competitor

I am in a mission called 'family
gather'; of course I will be the father
as the children will come on the way;
my report says you should be their
mother

And once we are together I shall teach
the children, despite that I could be
better, it is their mother who should
always matter

Sometimes I wonder how beautiful the
children will be

See, I can see that far so don't
mistake me for a player

I am your unemployed life time servant
just if your life is a city I am the
permanent mayor

I know you think I am imaginary and
funny but baby it is your fault because
my feelings for you makes me crazy

I am so impressed with your everything,
from yourself to your dressing, smile
to anger and when I see you shouting
like thunder I hear it is a piano
playing with no intrusion

I like that stubborn nature of yours
because for what is worth I don't think
it will interfere

By saying all that my point is simple
and clear, have me a chance to be yours
to perish each other's nightmares,
unfold our desires and for all the ups
and downs to have them together forever
experienced

HOW LOVE TAKES ME

I always knew love will come and find
me someday

But never did I know it will be you who
was heading on the way

And I can't have it in any further
delay

These are our lives linking like true
lovers meeting in a play

It is not about finding the perfect
person but it is about learning to see
the imperfect person perfect

We all have our flaws but when I see
you with my heart, perfection is all I
see

The same way when I look into your eyes
I capture you off guard and take you by
surprise

And I feel cool like some actor, like
James Bond in our love never dies

If life is a game, you are my favorite
dice

Lovers are like cloth and you are my
only size

It is true that all beauty and
perfection is from the above

You are presented to me as a well
packaged gift full of humor,
intelligence, beauty and love

From the way you laugh to when you are
upset, I love each thing that you do

I know with you all the troubles we
will get through

I know as long as we are on the same
journey together, we shall survive
whatsoever the storm and the yet to be
discovered weather

Have my word, to leave you will be
never, to love you will be ever, to be
there for you will be forever

To my lord I surrender, and I believe
he has made you to me as a favor

There is nothing that we cannot
achieve, so honey, worry shouldn't be a
bother

Sometimes I wonder of what we want is
too good to be true and I get scared to
get my heart broken and scared just by
the thought of loosing you

But in the end my heart says to move
further and faster

Not to be with you is as worse as to
lose you

I don't know about tomorrow but I know
you are mine today

I am fine by myself, too comfortable
with what I had but you make me work
just harder

The way you speak when you ask
something from me, I know it is
trickery but I am a blind man who
pulled out his own eyes

My friends say that I have changed;
they say I have gone soft

They say a woman has made unavailable,
she has made me busy just for herself

Isn't this what they say? That we
should all follow our hearts or maybe
my heart is throwing me away

I once ago left my home town with
borrowed money just for you and you had
sneaked out of the boarding school

I know I would never do that for
anybody else in the world because it
would be simply insane but with you it
was totally reasonably cool.

I AM ABOUT TO TELL YOU

Watch me when I stop by and look at me
in the eye because I am about to tell
you are the garden in the sky

You are my drug please do take me high

You are my wings; with you see how well
I can fly

Don't be so shy, you are already mine

And I have no intentions to make you
ever cry

I hope my affections will always
satisfy

Much that you will be incapable to lie

And some way you will have to believe I
am the only one to be in your heart
till we both die

Whatsoever your heart desires, I shall
comply

Believe it or not, you are sweater than
any pie

You have transformed me into a thinker
because I regularly wonder why I am
such fortuned to have you by my side

What are the forces that put us abide?

What is it so important that to lose
you has made me feel afraid?

You are quite a virus to my brain; you
have dominated my entire mind

You protrude my innervations and
upgrade my innovation

They should see what I see, beautiful
indeed you are, you are a masterpiece
creation

I have fallen in love with you by will
but I didn't meet you with intention

You may now not understand what I am
saying but some day you will know why I
admire our collaboration

Let it bring what it has to bring, let
it cost what it was meant to cost but I
know my heart is in the right place

There no much I can offer, I can only
do what I am supposed to do just like a
soldier

And I have the order which is to love
you has to not ever get over

Till somewhere deep in your heart you
admire I am more than Casanova

And that the bond we hold is more
powerful than a supernova

Too strong that if we dare separate we
shall both experience a psychotic
trauma

That can even make a person go to comma

Because you are my love, my eve and I
am the Adam that you shall only have

You are my fruit only by God you are
planted

You are my food; no drought can make me
hungry

You are my heaven on earth

You are meant to bring me happiness
even after my death

You are the finest color and if I have
color blindness then I don't want to be
okay

To me you are my soul mate, it doesn't
matter what they have to say

Because they would want me to leave my
world while they can never offer me a
better place to stay

As wild life is, I swear to be your
Tarzan

I will protect you from the evil world,
even from Satan

Let love make us before we make it

And when we do make love, we should
make sure it is the best memory of joy
there to be felt

I WANT YOU BACK

I don't know of your perception as you
hardly have with me the communication

So I usually go with the guessing to
have the information

But I need you to talk to me, honey, I
don't receive revelation

I know every couple got its fights and
this is out state of confusion

And maybe I happen to say a lot when I
was mad but leaving you has never been
my intention

Every time I think of you I get to cry
please save me from the tension

If love pays with time, I can wait for
the pension

But just come back my queen and don't
leave me is my only condition

Strongly binding together and we go
beyond the expectations

And stall tall exceeding the heights of
our imaginations

Cross over all the boundaries and all
the limitations

But I ask you not to love as before
because I need some addition

As I hope the me in you isn't under
deletion

Come one love, why can't we just have
the negotiation

Because our chemistry has great
reaction of a well balanced equation

The match we have cannot be sort by any
calculation

As now I know you are my perfection
without you my world isn't in
completion

My beautiful woman, can't you see for
you I am in some addiction

Your small neglects cause me into
frustration and soul infestation

The situation I am in takes me away
from concentration

For these painful days I rarely notice
the effects of earth's rotation

Come back my love, this is all I wish
to mention

For all the things I would want to say
this does the justification

You in my world is the best decoration

So please come back and end the
complication

Let's fight for our love and never go
about separation

We are so better together and to hell
with all the destructions

I will love you every tomorrow and that
needs no preparation

And if it wasn't for God, I feel before
you I would do the prostration

Anything for your happiness I am
waiting for your instructions

Please stop the entire act and let's
live our love story's endless extension

LOVE AT FRESH START

Hello, the ways you make me feel I
swear nobody has made me feel this
before

You absence affect my everything, be it
my mind, my heart and soul

Sometimes I wish I let it go before you
break my heart and end up saying I
should have done so

I am afraid that one day you will tell
me you have to go while with you old I
want to grow

But I love you very much that I cannot
give up and that you know

So no need to rush, let's take it slow,
with you I don't think there is such
thing as more

This melody makes me feel sentimental
and this love makes me feel low

And there is so much intensity that I
want it to stop

But this feeling that makes me
emotional, determinant makes me flow

I know you say you are different but
that's how it all starts

At the end they all say sorry it
couldn't work

I hope you prove otherwise because I
need the bite not the usual barks

I know right now you say I am like a
gift from above but look into my eyes
and tell me you see loads of love

And be afraid that you love me less and
that I am more than you deserve

Say loud to the world that in all your
life you will be the clouds and your
love rains upon me

You are the star of my little world, my
entire astronomy

That I am all that you love, in your
world I am at the top, not the stairs
or the balcony

Listen to my words they are from my
heart

It is you I solely love; I want you to
be mine for eternity

Not for a short while, that is
something I am tired of

It is alright you to prefer Dumbledore
and I prefer Gandalf

But the dramas and mood swings,
separations and arguments, honey please
spare me the unnecessary catastrophes

It can never be perfect but I have no
intention no matter the situation to
have myself from this love a doff

Let we make sure it goes on just as it
started.

MY AGENDA

This is from East Africa, a place
called Tanzania close to Kenya and
Uganda where my love for you became my
agenda

You are my beautiful courtesy; with you
I have no other priority

If fate is unwritten then ours was our
best decision

That smile on your face, that gorgeous
waist, they turn my mind restless

That shallow breath which you give
wherever I have you kissed, it makes me
irreversibly obsessed

Oh mother confessor, you have me under
your compulsion that I cannot overcome
such unwillingness

But I don't want it to go because it
gives me happiness

You are the witch without a wand

You are the magic of the words and
hands

We are so bonded together like the sea
and the sand

As pure as you are, I am a genuine
brand

I presume you aren't the propaganda but
the best of the wonder

As poisonous as you are, you are black
mamba

As vast in my heart, you are the
anaconda

More beautiful than the moon, in the
darkness you are my sun

Wherever I go, I want you by my side

Like the shadow that doesn't disappear
even with absence of light

When I see you my hearts gets to blow
and words begin to flow.

Suppose I am as well your light that is
the moment to glow

And this is for you to know, to let you
go is definitely no

This is no flirting, this is the
ultimate expression

To my world you are the queen, to my
happiness you are the key

For everything that has to be, your
presence is the greatest mystery

Let us spend more than a day together;
your presence is like the wanted
weather

Destiny is a road then ours is linked
forever

NUMBER ONE

You are my number one, whether you are
deep in the sand you are always in my
mind

You found me fresh and kind; you caught
me off guard and took me by surprise,
magically without a wand

Whether you are someone else's or mine,
being with you is like travelling in
time

I loved you when love was truly blind
and I didn't care to see what is there
to come

Don't be surprised I am still in love;
don't be shocked I still want you
around

Your voice can still turn me upside
down

You can't blame me for seeing you
beautiful as a dove, you are quite of a
design

We understand each other without saying
anything like a glimpse on destiny

As strangers meet in some place in a
town not knowing how things will turn
out

I have called you my queen; it is by my
heart I did put on you my crown

I have called you my key; you are the
opener of my happy world

May be I wasn't perfect but I had deep
faith of what was about to come about

You may try to hide it but I can see
through your eyes and fortunately you
know I can

I am not such a past as you want it to
look like

Just feel the words; a lot will come in
mind

When we meet at home or downtown, there
is that feeling of needing a hug

May be that is the past but the heart
knows otherwise

I am not asking to change what has
happened but I am asking to drop the
fight

Because not everything hidden truly
stays out of sight

This could be simply art, the bribery
of words but it is very true you are my
number one and I cannot have that
denied

Your exploding body makes me feel less
holy

Seeing you makes me jolly

Maybe I wish for a kiss or a hug or
anything of sort but it is hard to know
what I want the most

Perhaps destiny isn't on our side but I
am certain we have chemistry

And I know why you think of me as a
mystery

Falling in love doesn't make the loved
one a criminal,

Don't think I forged our lives into a
story for it was something out of hand

It could be you found me a little bit
lost but heart was still a pure brand

And so much has happened, a few has
changed but I still call you darling

I still mention your name with respect

I don't know if it is love or undying
crush but I enjoy it most of the time

It freshen my mind when I picture our
days, when we could chat the whole day
and tall all night long

Nothing ever seemed wrong; nothing was
boring enough to become old

The crowd has never been told but my
dear, you were and you are one of the
kind

With the way you are charming, it could
take me to wonderlands

I miss you and I don't know why

When you have this read then know you
are truly my number one.

TELL ME

It happens like how it always done, as
they all start as is later becomes was

When a broken heart gets re-broken

When the beautiful moments turn to into
wars

When the one who did matter the most
leaves you with sores

Each time another one approaches, gives
you the same hope for something better

But at the end they bring pain,
sometimes even more

Until you chose to believe there is no
such thing as love

And yet you cannot see you are a victim
of something you claim it doesn't exist

I am telling you this because with you
I am in love

And I am done saying no to myself

Just because I am afraid to face a
betrayal, it doesn't withstand the fact
you have become irresistible

I won't rush showing you the much I
love you as in such I play low

Until you show me to you what is my
heart for?

Do you really intend to become the
partner of my soul?

Do you really want me to be for
eternity your heart's store?

Or you just want this to be one of the
'it happened once ago'?

Look at me; you can see through my eyes
the love for you I hold

Tell me you can see I need more than
what you have me told?

Because you are the key and my
happiness is the door

For the depth of love I have for you,
we both know I cannot let you go

Tell me; you don't want me for show

Show me darling I am the great person
you know

Tell me you want me to marry you and
not to date you

Tell me I am the person of your
tomorrow

Tell me love, the love we have is like
blood and I am the vessel in which they
flow

Tell me you shall not befall upon my
heart tournaments of sorrow

Tell me each day you will love me more

Tell me you won't throw me when old
when I grow

THE GIRL I FOUND

I have looked for true love in all ways
till with you I have seen the sign

For my eyes you surely do them an
amaze, I hope you know what I am saying

I swear I have seen pretty faces but
you turn me crazy like cocaine

When I say you are the only woman my
heart cares, I hope you know I am not
lying

Deep inside I melt but I pretend I am
all fine

The way I last for your gaze, for all
the pleasures of the world I will
bargain

You don't have to guess, my thoughts
you contain

To your love I fear to be a slave untie
me from such addictive chains

The more the days, the more you are my
wine

I have become easy to trace as your
love is a beautiful stain

You make my heart race, you make my
head spine

You are all over my head, you have
possessed my brain

This love is so craze, I ask you to
save me from this pain

My feelings for you are nonstop, you
are my heart's admin

You have become my sun rays, the one
who makes my heart burn

You are such hot, you are such a blaze
but I rejoice the union

My life is less and you are all I need
to gain

I hope our bond is to forever ties and
marriage the chain

My heart on your hands it lies, don't
have it dined

I am not sure if I have yours but soon
I hope to make it mine

Believe it sweetheart, I mean to be
more than end of days or an endless
phase

You don't have copies; to me you are
the only one

This is what my heart says and if you
don't get it I can do it once again

THE ONE I NEED

Have me a place in your life I will
make it perfect like a film

It won't be named vampire diary

It will be 'the man who is lovely'

And you shall make a better star than
Hale Berry

Because you are my black berry

With you I have the BBM

You are my fairly

That travels like light beam

In advance I say sorry

For any pain I might cost our dream

It is you I want to marry

To have my life redeemed

YOU ARE

Hey my queen

To my soul you are its twin

My witch

Your magic has made me better than I
have ever been

Hey my day dream

You are all that I deem

If you are destined for one love

Let me be him

You are my sleep

Of which I don't want to wake up

You are my sit

On which I don't want to stand up

YOU'VE NOWHERE ABOUTS

This is a knockout without a punch

This is an accident without an event

This is costly without a price

This is love and you're the loved one
and I am the one loving you and you
have no whereabouts

I wish at least you say hi, I wish at
least you look at me when you pass by,
I wish you smile at me when you happen
to look into my eyes

I think about you than my own well
being, I am being obsessed with you
that I cannot lie

This love is killing and for you I
shall die

And you are my killer but you aren't
aware of the homicide

And if I survive, by heart you should
know I am crazy over you and that I
cannot deny

The problem is, I run speechless and
you are all shy

I am all free less, damn I wish I cry

You gave me no chance to prepare,
please give me a chance to try

Because when you are around my
adrenaline makes me want to fly

As much as I want to show you what I
feel, for your image only I rely

Please keep coming by, you are such a
beauty that makes me want to say 'Oh
my!'

I cannot get used to you, the fault
isn't mine

I have loved before; this feels like
the one I felt once in a time

You must be the chosen one for this is
an almost forgotten feeling to my heart

You seek no permission, you seek no
warrant all you do is have me the
desire to see you more

You aren't any girl; you must be my
destined amour

For these unique feelings you give my
heart I hope I am by the side of your
soul

And soon I shall have to put the end to
this all

Not that I shall love you no more but
to the next level to get this go

I promise you nothing in that than I
intend to give you what I myself don't
know

It will be too much, too big, too
beautiful that you will not be able to
hold

In love you should fall

Helplessly until you turn me into your
mentor

Not that I am any special but my love
is

Just don't chuck me away; this is your
only way to know

Whoever broke your heart before doesn't
matter because I have as well been
broken once

I am not going to rewrite your story,
this is a fresh start made only for you
and I

But how can I do that while I turn
wordless when I see you around

When you throw a gaze on my eyes how
will I be able to just do that?

I at the moment fantasize you being
mine but the fact is I don't know where
to even start

This is a knockout without a punch;
this is an accident without an event,
this is costly without a price, this is
love and you're the loved one and I am
the one loving you and you have no
whereabouts

FOR MAMA

Your love for me has grown in time,
from the last summers to this summer,
from this summer to any summer

The one whom your pain forsake me like
a severe tumor

You are admirable mama, so much that I
generatively acknowledge you than my
own humor

You have lived in time as the one with
my greatest honor

The first time I live I was within you
and everything I had you were my donor

As this love will always live longer
even after our lives have surpassed
their timers

How is possible to love you enough
while you loved me long before I can
remember?

That woman that I love, that daughter
that I so much care about, you exceed
them perhaps because you are more than
I deserve

My number one queen, make a sound of
need, I shall be there to serve

The one whom by fate, I am your
descendant

You made me so important that when
raising me you never wanted assistance

You knew no one can take care of me
better

Thank you for all that you did for me,
you are doing for me and those that you
will do for me

I love you compassionately my dear mama

I hope you know your love hasn't
existed without its true admirer

CHAPTER THREE: SAD OR HEART BROKEN

MINE SOUL

Hold still mine soul, I promise you
these tragedies you will overcome them
all

I would want you to be strong because
they could be worse tomorrow

I have wronged you so much, forgive me,
your grief has been quite of a
punishment

Sometimes you wish I let you go because
those times you wonder what this life
is for.

Have faith the storm will pass, the
grieve will vanish

Be patient my soul, thy lord will make
your pain perish

I know you are tired of breaking the
laws it is time to tell the devil 'no'

Trust in thy God, he is the one far
more aware of the impact of your goals

I know you have so many things for me
to establish but my dear there some
impurities in you that you must abolish

Please hold still mine soul for your
lord surely knows

He has been aware of your false before
they could cost and your glory before
it could astonish

I am sorry for the pain that I have
brought you but you are the one who
always hold the door

Life is made of a lot, sometimes the
sad story, sometimes that which truly
flourish

Your power is my strength; open your
eyes my soul let me see what you can
see

You have the power to make me feel the
snow while it is sunny and the sun
while there is snow

I know I am asking a lot after what you
have gone through

You are the partner that God gave me,
don't tell me what I believe in you
isn't true

Stay calm from within

Find the true potential that you are
blessed with

Even if it will cost me to bleed,
cutting into pieces you will just grow
again like a tree

I am the body and I do, you are the
soul and you will

Prosper in your imagination and let me
do the things that yourself won't
believe

Behold mine soul and know God never
deceives

You are lost in mistakes and sorrow and
your happiness is ceased

I pray your lord helps your power be
retrieved

And I am the one telling you it is all
going to be fine while that has always
been your job

You let me cry but I am happy this also
makes me pray

I ask God to forgive you, you have made
me commit sins and I know it is
pointless to say it is the devil

Trust in your lord mine soul, he
forgives even what cannot be perceived

For he is the kindest, open the door to
him and let the wonders channel
themselves

The light from him will purify you and
you will grieve no more

So hold still mine soul, these
tragedies you will overcome them all

I know you are frightened with the
horrors of the future; you are scared
of what it could bring

Be patient mine soul, let me do what
you tell me and worry less of what it
is to come

Because when you are sad, broken or
down, I cannot do my best

I need you strong my soul, you're the
elementary block of my wall, please
don't tremble it down

And sometimes it is just not in your
hand, the pain doesn't mean anything
but the fact you have accepted things
to bring you down

Have faith in the working of the lord,
be brave, be calm and let me heal our
world

I AM SORRY

You can be mad for a moment but don't threaten me to stay apart

I am not aware of the days and nights with you out

I am sorry for the mistakes I have made; I have never intended to hurt

Of course without you I can survive but to live oh no I can't

I won't commit suicide; it is just that my life is becoming worthless as dust

You are my happiness, my wife an essential of my life

I cannot give you everything you ask but I can be all you ever dreamt about

You are my boss; you don't need permission to check on me, no need of a warrant

I haven't been very open about your role in my life, I am sorry if I have made you feel insignificant

You are a person that no matter how much I don't praise, you can never turn to irrelevant

I am at your service, I am your servant

My love for you exists be it we are
close or distant

You push my will power, your needs make
me brilliant

I cannot always do it at instant but I
want you to know I will do all that I
can and try all that I cannot

You are my super woman, my wonder woman

Love me enough; forgive me already
those are my wishes and they needs your
grant

I am sorry for the times I didn't
compliment on your makes ups, food or
dresses

And I would like you to know you are my
beautiful woman in whatever size you
are, be it slim, average or fat

It is you I dream about despite it is
you I always had, I need you more than
you can possibly doubt

My ornament please my love cooperate

You are everything I want, for such
shortcoming please tolerate

I know they hunt please for me don't be
caught

In my heart you are dominant; I shall
love you more than constant

Sweetheart, you are my coefficient, for
your love I am dependant

You are my beloved accident, a
wonderful gift like a parent

With all the shatters that can happen
in life, I ask you to be the most
opposite

Don't be over modest, correct me when I
am incorrect

I am sorry baby and let's rewind it so
it may be better than the start

I CAN'T BE WITH YOU

I can see it when you look at me; I
know you mean it when you say it to me

But love is no trade, hurting you is
all that is going to be

I know you say that you need me and
that is because you too much love me

But I don't feel the same, pretending
isn't my tradition

At the end I shall break your heart
into pieces and you shall blame for
something you enforced it to be

I know you hope you shall win me, I am
not saying I am one of the kinds

It could be you are just overestimating
your skills to win a heart

If I suggest we be friends, you say you
don't want me as a friend

But it is worth it, friends can be
entitled to love without quarrels

Maybe you shall win me through it but I
cannot promise you that

Not because I don't want it but because
I don't feel it

By the way this could be a test if you
are true, a player's patience only
softens his or her heart unknowingly so
I don't mind you waiting

I should confess I love when you speak
love to me

It flatters me and makes me feel
special and for that I cannot push you
away; you are like a hug that I need
despite you give me a heck of time to
make you understand me

But don't overdo it because it becomes
annoying or pressuring

I am not doing this because I was hurt
before but because I don't want to hurt
you as we go

It crosses my mind to be friends with
benefit but that is to take advantage
of you

Making you feel like I love you while
it isn't true

And if I were you I would have felt
like a fool

I wonder what I am to say to you than
move on but don't stop loving me

I know it is crazy but love doesn't
come everyday

Maybe I shall remember you when I feel
lonely

I know you are sexy and tempting, many
people's choice

Or at least that is what you think of
yourself

I admire you but it is just that I
cannot be with you

And I think it is for the good that
comes as bad like robin coming in his
hood

So don't insist until my heart permits

I cannot be with you because I feel
sorry for you because at the end I
shall feel sorry for myself

So if you want to be with me, just try
to win me

But don't hope coz it may not turn as
the way you want it to be

I am sorry to say these but it is
necessary to face it

DON'T WORRY ABOUT ME

It is alright that you don't feel the
same

It is not that I don't have feelings
for you anymore

Neither is it that I don't give a damn

It is only I have accepted that there
is nothing to me you owe

It hurts yes but in that there is no
shame

Despite all the hopes, somewhere in me
I knew I am was just an arrow and love
was the bow

It was just a matter of time before it
threw me away, make me so lame

I had a thought with how beautiful you
are; if you were mine it would make a
perfect crow

But don't worry, that was just a cover,
I never loved you for fame

You say I am a good guy, you wish I was
the one you firstly saw

Don't worry about me; I cannot have you
under blame

I have made peace long with how you
feel for me my dear, just let me keep
trying to lay low

I am content with who you are to me,
some days I will find someone who
loving me is all she will claim

I love you in anyway there is, may you
always know

REMEMBER

I remember when I use to catch you
staring at me and then pretend that you
weren't

And when you would try to check to see
if I am still looking at you, you find
me still staring with a growing smile
that you fail not to reply it with a
smile

I can remember when you couldn't talk
after realizing that I am close

And at distant you would smile and
offer gestures my eyes have yet seen

My love, I freshly remember when I did
tell you how much I love you

You couldn't help but crying in front
of me, the tears I have never
understood

You kissed me and hugged me, I carried
you up and you opened your arms as if
you were flying

As I brought you down, you said that
you love me too and kissed my chick and
hugged me once again

I remember the second day; I held your arm against my racing heart and told you

"They are such unstable beats due to your presence and that each one carries your name in it"

You hugged me shyly and said with your pretty smile

"I would let you touch my heart too except you will be touching something else"

I remember when we danced under the rain, the dance with no music, no steps only our crazy love

I remember when you would be mad at me because I didn't reply your texts or pick you up on time

I by heart also remember that day you told me you love me so much but you cannot be with me because you are supposed to marry another person

I remember how I couldn't understand you, filled with rage and you tried to keep me calm but it couldn't work

A few days when my mind was back, I tried to reach you but you weren't

reachable until when a friend of yours
told me the next day was the wedding

I remember when I tried to cheer up but
nothing could help, I remember every
dime of it, every pain my heart
indulged

So as a lover, reality says one thing
but the heart keeps dreaming like there
is still hope for it to be true again

The memories that you have installed in
my mind have made me express the best
words yet that I could

So much of memories that I don't know
if you will ever be a memory to my sad
heart

I hope as you live happily with your
life, some place you find homage in
remembering me too

Not for any promise, just for the sake
of making all the joy we had was not
entirely meaningless

Remember, that is all I ask!

GOT NOTHING TO LOOSE

I bet you think you are looking for a
better person, the kind that isn't even
there

You just changed my fate, broke my
heart and filled my eyes with tears

My once sweet dream has turn into a
nightmare

Maybe you are doing this because you
think I will always be here

You may be my so called love, beloved
dear but you aren't my entire happy
share

You may not appreciate what I bare but
out there, there is someone who will
tell me loosing me is all that she
fears

So gather your strength while I can
still wait because soon I shall leave
you with only things to remember

If I had destroyed your life, you have
the rights to be sincere

You can just tell me to let go if you
think your happiness is all what I
hinder

That I have brought you tragedies and
blocked the things that you could have
achieved

I will understand that he is a real
deal and I am an old folder

May be he is a boy wonder but keep in
mind, you are just increasing the
number

And soon you shall realize he isn't the
one who invented love

Don't mistake this for a beg

It was once in a time to your love I
had surrender

I may have fragments of concern but it
is a limited care

You can't treat me as your teddy bear
and you don't pick my calls, you do
nothing and still you want it to sound
fair

Go, you are so important to me but not
as my air

Sure I was your lover but to me you
were a partner.

And on the way you may have stopped
seeing it going far, far enough for us
to be grandparents

My feelings to you was my comfort but
now it is the source of disaster

The storm you have brought to my heart
isn't meant for a person to bear

But I will surprise you how well I can
walk on fire

I will heal the wounds, not even one I
will have it speared

These wounds that you caused me, they
will leave you surprised how much the
power of anger can take over the power
of soft desires

You will be surprised enough to figured
out your expectation is a liar

And upon your own plan I turn as the
plan grandmaster

You can know you succeeded to hurt me a
little bit but to yourself it will be
magnified

Do not lie to yourself that you will
forget, memories aren't as controllable
to chose what to and what not to
remember

If you feel threatened, it isn't my
fault

You only estimated me for being less
strong

I know what you are doing and you will
be a subject of your own game

Baby, you just can't get me toyed, you
just can't get me played

Because you need to know I got nothing
to lose.

HOPE TO MEET YOU

I cannot work, I cannot think and all
this is because of what I am feeling

How do you expect me to be okay if you
are nowhere near me?

Love has cursed a curse upon me,
without you how can I love again?

The thoughts of you have become my
shadow, spare me just for today

The world has become hell to me, I wish
I lived on the moon for there I will
stop thinking I will see you soon

This is a heavy burden, a great storm

Loving is breathtaking but missing is
consuming

Forgive me, if I have been so
persistent

It isn't my fault if I still hope one
day I shall be your groom

That one day I shall carry you inside
our new home

And give you all that I can give from
the first day and you will be surprised
how well I can go on

You are mine to love but you aren't
mine to be with

You left me in the middle of nowhere;
somewhere life is so cold, cold enough
to freeze

For your love, hope still breaths

And has always been healthy enough to
overcome all the diseases

I am not asking you to feel sorry; I am
saying you being away have made my life
a sad story

I am telling you, you are loved than
ever before

I am telling you in love you made me
fall.

My hopes are mine alone, I still I can
still write a few sad lines

Because if I neglect it, nothing of
goodness my mind can design

I am all good but I am moving on not
very fine

But I wish you lots of happiness, it is
a wish I had ever since the day upon
you I laid my eyes till the day I can't
see you no matter how hard I would try

I dearly hoped that I married you
before you departed this world

And I am telling you this on your grave
hoping you will hear it all

I am hoping that you hear for the sake
of my voice and for the tears that fall
as I speak

Just to remind myself it is not
anybody's fault

I always wonder how easily people just
turn I love to I loved because someone
passed

Oh my love it is not that I am still
grieving, it is that I still love you

I dearly pray God keep you safe; I hope
you are somewhere safe.

I love you persistently my love and I
hope to meet you soon.

THE ETERNAL LOVE

At a distance I see you my star,
wonderful as you are it doesn't matter
how far

It feels so good looking at you;
suppose you are an art then you are a
masterpiece

You are a great view that tells beauty
is true

But it breaks my heart to know I shall
never be with you

When I remember the day I met you,
looking into your eyes, you looking
into mine that seeming childish love
took my heart away

You were too beautiful to me that
wherever you were close my heart would
jump its beats

I would run speechless and the only
thing I could do is staring at you

You mattered to me than how you can
possibly think

You are the world I never had; you are
the melody only my heart could sing

I miss you my dear though I had to
accept you are never meant to be mine,
my heart is still having that
difficulties understanding that

I might be young to be such open to
love you but I was never young to fall
in love with you

You knew you had more than a space in
my heart but all you didn't know is how
huge that space is

By the way, it is all the heart

I had always loved loving you because
it inspired to have a great future that
I could live it with you

But my love you were already setting
your thoughts into some other future

The future you are in now that doesn't
involve me

You let me fall deeper in love as if
you wanted to spend the rest of your
life with me breaks my heart even more

I cannot complain about this and I wish
it was just as a lesson but the truth
it is an illness no treatment can help

And honey you have no any idea about
this

I am sorry I call you babe, the very
names I called you then, I am simply
used to loving you

Though I never had the experience of
you loving me than those blushes, gazes
and heartwarming promises and that you
love me being on the top

Now I hate loving you

I want to let you go so badly but I
fail especially when I pretend you are
a past to me

I don't need a love story to remind me
what love is because I have you in mind
daily

This is frustrating, each time I close
my eyes and sit somewhere alone I see
you my star

When I open my eyes and look aside
hoping to see you, my eyes drop sad
tears

I mourn over no funeral, oh please
honey be here

Losing you was all I ever truly feared

Now I am just a sad lover proving
everyday you are to my heart eternal

And I just hope this isn't the end

THAN BEAUTIFUL

Those days when she came so close to me
and I couldn't resist it because I
liked it had exposed her to me enough
to consider her part of me

Without knowing this will cause an
impression and some impressions ignite
some feelings, I just wish I knew.

At any cost she treated me well that
her own peace of mind and every time I
noticed it that it was more than she
said it I choose to cover it with
friendship

But sneaky little love has grown big in
her heart

I wasn't in love with her and still I
couldn't take it back

Because I never saw the kind of beauty
I wanted in her, I believed I didn't
feel a thing than friendship

But on the other hand she was totally
lost for me

My heart was her home that she was so
desperate to be in it

And of course she hoped the hopes that
I couldn't offer

But mercy grew in me I had to
reconsider her

She was a nice lady, lovely and
pleasant, she knew me well and had true
desire to treat me the best

I didn't want to take any advantage;
all I wanted was to play my role of
justice as I called it

And I believed I have to force myself
to love her

Every day was hard to act in love until
it was very poor for her to notice

She decided to take her heart into
nobody's hands coz the man she loved
the most had torn it badly

Though she tried to begin afresh with
someone else, her recollections with me
were her most precious thing she ever
had

Turning to myself loneliness woke me up
so I tried to win her back again

At times I told myself it is because I
enjoyed to be loved and I miss it

Sometimes I tell myself it is justice
to try to give her happiness again

But the truth is, these days made me
realize that she was of course not
beautiful to me but she was more than
beautiful to my heart no matter how
much I never acknowledged that

Now she has resisted coming back at the
moment I am over weighed with
admiration upon her

It is seriously hard to find some like
her, at least like her

There is nobody to replace her

By then joy blinded me but now pain has
awaken me

I admit I love her with an overdo

No matter what anybody would say, I
find her absolutely beautiful

"THANK YOU"